Merry Christ
from
Ned Conque
15 December 2004



7

# Lays and Legends of Virginia and Otherwhere

Poems

By Ned Conquest

THE APOLLONIAN PRESS

Richmond, Va. Washington, D.C.

Apollonian Press Edition, 29 May 2004



Printed and published in Richmond, Va. and Washington D.C.
The United States of America



Library of Congress Catalog Number 2003 190104

ISBN 0-9627485-4-4

To my brother,
Henry Fairfax Conquest

The social, friendly, honest man,
Whate'er he be,
'Tis he fulfills great Nature's plan,
And None but he!

— Robert Burns

# Lays and Legends of Virginia And Otherwhere

## Part I. Queen Mab Subjects

**Part II. Responses, Wry and Reverent**



**Part III. Greek and Roman Graces**

## Part IV. Woolly Willy Speaks His Mind



## Part V. Some Legends of Virginia

Part I.

# Queen Mab Subjects

## Queen Mab Subjects

Come, thou fairy mid-wife,
        All too seldom sung, —
Dip in flesh thy finger,
        Touch my burning tongue.

On dreams — remembered yearnings! —
        Come, feed my fiercest hour:
Wrapped in opium whispers,
        Lead me to thy bower.

I bless thy fevered presence,
        Thou, my god supreme:
Thine the soul's awaking,
        Thine the sleep of dream!

Come, raze the palsied idols
        That all my senses keep —
Come, thou fairy mid-wife,
        Death-defying sleep!

## God Takes a Ship

"… Men ne cunnon
secgan tō sōðe, selerǣdende,
hæleð under heofenum, hwā þǣm hlæste onfēng."
— *Beowulf*

*"… No one knows,*
*to tell the truth – dwellers in hall,*
*heroes under the heavens – who received that burden."*

I remember night and the moonlight breaking,
Shivering cobblestones
Over the swan road,
Arched by gleaming
Dolphin-back—

And the frightened whiteness,
Brief, triangular,
Off to the knife-edge
Weld of world,
Bright below a sea-black sky —

And who, and what? And why was it lifting
Canvas wing
Over indigo deep?
Why but to taste the star-dark lip —
Who but a lover to kiss the sky?

## The Sleeping Horses of Thorvaldsen

*Sculpture seen in Copenhagen, 1957*

Endless archways, twilight-framed,
Shear their whiteness from the night –
Hold them, beasts emulsified,
Broken to the sad solution,
Gray museuming silence.

Leaning listless, shadow-stalking,
Into the face of midnight turned,
There they draw their ghost-filled breath
And wait – as if for a darker dark,
As if for the last, long ringless ride.

Night must hold their polished presence,
Night and the moon's marmoreal stare –
Not the prick of a proud ear forward,
Not a hint of their sunlit stride,
Nothing dims their dull repose.

Only legs of the most alive –
Bone-filled boots Apocalyptic! –
Only the end can break to life
The trunk-like limbs of these long monsters,
Beasts beyond the pride of burden.

## Aubade

Aubade, O song of lovers,
        Sung when they part at dawn –
Oh hold my, hear my stillness,
        Heart of a heart that's gone.

O bod, O song of the Father,
        Sung when He'd finished all –
Oh hold my, host my restless
        Seed of a living fall.

Aubade, O worse, O worsening,
        Rib of a sleep-starved side –
Oh have my, hive my teeming
        Sweet of a queen-clad pride.

Aubade, O grim perfection,
        Sung to a milking thigh –
Oh hang my hope, my always
        Harp, on a new-born cry!

## Though the more abundantly I love, the less I be beloved

I want your born
Your bursting sun
I want your cling
I want your sky

I want your prayed
Your star-gold hope
I want your with
I want your now

I want your gone
Your breast-fed youth
I want your lisped
I want your grow

I want your dreamt
Your self-sung lie
I want your failed
I want your done

I want your gave
Your treasured then
I want your hurt
I want your die

I want your lived
Your happied all
I want your want
I want my own

## The Passing of a Heathen Dog

Ignoble beast! Rat-tailed ribald!
He won't bemire my rug
Or chew a table leg again. —
He'll never sow my hearth with dusty dinge of hair
Or crust my cuff with dewlap dew.
He'll never praise the paint off cellar doors
In hungry, claw-filled, panting black salaams.
He'll never shine my walls with rain-sweat
Shaken in that blurring, rustling roar of street-soaked hide.
He'll never maul another shoe,
Or roll me berry-brown eye from under shredded newsprint.
He'll never thump the house awake at midnight —
Make us marvel at the haunch power
Of his grim, flea-fetching fury.
I'm rid, I know, of all that's wrong about the house —
And yet, he'll never lick my hand again.

## Confession

I used to sing while I was at it:
How silently, how silently the world becomes the white!
Oyster shells are pearling, and day forgets the night! ...
I always loved the snow: it meant for most a God-kissed day of rest.
I was a second-storey man, and rain was all right
(Except it made roofs slippery) because it washed away
The fingerprints of feet. Snow, on the other hand –
A piece of vellum holding the confession
To which you simply put your mark.
But snow would always court me to some one else's house,
To stand astride an ermine-coated life without the pain of living.
In strange bedrooms I would rise to my vicarious best,
Feeling snow come down.
I didn't always steal. Sometimes I sat and held my breath
To think what other things had come to light
In that dark room of rooms.
Those were the gladdest hours! Dust-beard pictures, gap-toothed combs,
And mirrors, blind, would many a bureau haunt with me –
Sometimes leprous ashtrays fumed beside the bed,
And shameless bottles, brown beneath their gawdy labels –
The bed itself unmade (No one hopes to host a stranger here!)
Like all tomorrow's love and all today's –
Peeling walls the paint could never cotton to as much as I —
And closets full of empty clothes that often fit.
I didn't always steal. Like the last time I was caught –
Tracks in the snow on terrace and on roof: a calling card
Engraved by God, served smiling from a tray of inlaid pearl.
On the bed I sat, lightening some dark-bottomed bottle there,
Wearing a suit of those empty clothes,
Trying to hear the snow that curled like a cat's tail
Back and forth across the friendly window.
They found me a cell on the second storey of the jail.

## Contract

My handsome young fellow,
My beautiful lass,
Come live with me here
Till your flesh becomes grass –
But don't steal the produce,
Don't slander your pay,
Or I'll kill you forever
By night and by day.

All right! We will come –
For we haven't much choice –
We'll stay and we'll work
And we'll worship your voice!
Steal? – You won't know it;
Complain we will none;
And we'll keep to our place
Like the moon and the sun.

One word of good warning –
Though surly you are,
And if help wasn't scarce,
I'd boil you in tar –
That apple tree there,
Not a twig of it breaks!
Guard the fruit with your life,
And – beware of the snakes.

What? Snakes in this jungle?
Aren't *you* bad enough?
No union, no shop steward,
Only "huff-puff"?
We'll tend your old tree
Till each bough has salaamed –
(And double our take,
Or be both of us damned!)

## Song of the Modern Melchizedek

With bleeding foot
And cross of gold,
Wander I still
As I did of old –
With sniffing hook
And midnight locks,
The lifelong book,
The thousand shocks
That flesh and I are heir to.

Stay and hear
Of a thirsty hope,
Suckled on gall
And smoke and pope –
Stay and feel
The crumpled horn
Of a battered ram
Whose star unborn
Leads where the foot must fare to.

Hear and know
The bush must burn,
The flesh-full knife
Must sink and turn –
The gold must melt,
The lifeblood dry,
The wall must fall,
And Rachel cry:
But don't – unless you dare to.

Know and believe
That all is naught –
My house unbuilt,
My war unfought,
My home unfound,
My hope too great,
My will unbound,
My faith too late –
But only God will care to!

## The Holy Birth

Christmas morning,
Christ a-borning,
All the world and God adorning –
Sing Him, praise Him all the day!

Shepherds kneeling,
Christ revealing;
Pagan gods in tumult reeling –
Sing Him, praise Him all the day!

Trumpets sounding,
Grace abounding,
Love and life a kingdom founding–
Sing Him, praise Him all the day!

Tree-tops shining,
Christ divining,
Every heart and hearth refining –
Sing Him, praise Him all the day!

Magi bearing
Gifts of caring:
Hither come, and join the sharing –
Sing Him, praise Him all the day!

## A Prayer

O Lord, make me believe till true belief
Shall fill my emptiness with living soul;
Make hope my joy till joy shall turn to grief
That dullness clouded so my hoped-for goal.
O Lord, restrain my fears lest they be spent
Before, through tears, thy burning throne I see;
Teach me to thank till, at thy footstool bent,
E'vn thanks shall seem presumptuous in me.
O Lord, conceal my faults, not from thy sight,
But from my own red, desperate-fevered eye;
Forgive unwilling virtue which by right
Condemns itself for being half a lie.
O Lord, at my despair do not despair:
Blind not to thee one blind to all else fair.

## The First Judgment

No hole where we can hide from our own shame,
No fellow mind our wall-less prison to cheer,
No living thing but Hydra-headed fear!
And none but our own squirming selves to blame –
To blame for chains unseen by any eye,
For life-long scars we are afraid to show,
For penance only we can do and know,
For tears of soul-blood which unheard we cry.
O Fools, to hope for mercy in that court
Gray grim where jury, judge, and judged are one,
Where but to live our lives is to atone
And thought makes all life's joys the judge's sport!
O God, if torments such as these be past
With man's first judgment, must we fear the last?

## The Blessed Virgin's Appeal to the Jews

Wy haue yȝ no reuthe on my child?
Haue reuthe on me ful of murni(n)g,
Taket doun on rode my derworÞi child,
Or prek me on rode with my derling.

More pine ne may me ben don
Þan laten me liuen in sorwe & schame:
Als loue me bindet to my sone,
So lat us deyȝen boÞen i-same.

*-Religious Lyrics of the XIVth Century,*
*ed. Brown, Oxford, 1957.*

Why have ye no pity on my child?
Have pity on me then, as I mourn!
Take down from the cross my precious child
Or nail me there with my firstborn!

Greater wrong could not be done
Than make me live in sorrow, in shame:
As love still binds me to my son,
Treat us in death and life the same.

## Sunset on Calvary

Nou goth sonne under wod, —
me reweth, marie, Þi faire Rode.
Nou goÞ sonne under tre, —
Me reweÞ, marie, Þi sone and Þe.

— *English Lyrics of the XIIIth Century*
*ed. Brown, Oxford, 1962.*

Behind the wood now sets the sun, —
My shame, O Mary, has begun!
Beneath the tree the sun sinks low, —
Thy cross, thy son, and thee my woe.

## I Will Become a Friar

*Rendition of an English lyric of the XIIIth Century.*

No more will I so wicked be,
The world holds not my soul in fee:
Go, raiment wild; go, foolish glee!
    My face will now be glum.
A knotted rope my belt shall be;
    A monk I will become.

Myself a friar I will make,
Lechery I will forsake,
Myself to Christ I will betake –
    The church I will not shirk;
In all the hours I am awake
    God's will shall be my work.

I will but do this one good deed
For Him Who bought us in our need;
From out His side now flows my creed,
    So dear His blood was then!
In truth I am a mad-man freed
    Who reveled once in sin.

## The Lesson

"Whom seek ye?" said the Master;
And Mary, stricken dumb,
Replied, as to a gardener,
"Him who is to come."

In heart, though not in mouth,
She framed the words there then.
Said He, in holy truth,
"I *am* now come again!—

"But touch me not, save as
Your love has touched my own.
Tell all that I arise,
For now, to God alone."

And so she did; though none
Believed her wingéd words
Until, their own hope gone,
They flew on them like birds.

May ever learn we such
As what we heard of Mary:
By love alone we touch,
And God is hard to bury.

## Through Depths of Height

Blood sun and slate-blue sliding floor –
Airplane, god-like, sits its throne of cloud.

## To my Love in the Convent of Cities

Nightingale, nightingale, within your silver shrine,
Can you sing the windless death that wastes the mountain pine?
Can you sing the linden laughter, arching green in vain?
Or hymn the poplar's shivered whisper, pale as sunny rain?

## Evening Thoughts

To hear the owl's old song at night
Makes darker yet the blackest wood –
Of all the past puts out the light,
And mocks the morrow's good.

## From the Grave

*"... For what is man that he should live out the lifetime of his God?"*
*– Herman Melville*

The years have been in faith and not in vain:
What matters then the nothingness of now?
We had our God when it was good to have him,
When like a friend he lived beside us strong,
In Roman fashion deigning not our own
Death to survive. Could we ask more of any?
Of parent, wife, or yet life-drinking child?
Ah, *would* we ask – to share this last return
To dust and silence?

## A Lover, Dying Young

That you could be my sepulchre! –
Your brimming breast my pillow,
Your arms, your legs my crimson silk –
I, your melting pale Paolo, you my deep Francesca...
Only, let me curse you not:
If such eternity would punish you,
Let God forget my very name,
And leave me to the worst that I deserve.

## The End of the Road

Are we there, then – you and I?
No curse has stained that lip
Where yet my kisses live,
No wind of words
Has blown apart our hair –
But silent, separate here we lie,
And know the truth
Of time and touch
And ancient torture,
Born of the parting life –
Two brands, whose thought-infested dew
Lies low as the laughing flame
That all but sundered them.

## The Colleen Gone

Farewell, since you will have it,
Till blue leaves Irish eyes,
Till Blarney stones are kissed to dust
And lovers tell no lies.

Farewell, and take more with you
Than ever I could give
While we two lay together
And let our poor flesh live.

Farewell; I love, and tried to,
Though little it matters now:
A word unsaid, a hope unshared –
God teach both of us how!

## Late March Day

Fish-fleck gray,
And I'm inside –
Jonah in the belly
Of the sky!

A leaf, dry as April snakeskin,
Flying to find its lengthy way,
Borne on clear blue wind of winter –
We dare not hear its gentle search,
Touching glass like a lover's finger,
Fluttering forward, curling down,
Almost ashamed, almost alive.

Window panes a prison make,
Dungeoning sky outdoors –
Each last looming leaf bound down
To rebel soil and damp delay,
Happy slave
To the smell of spring in the wind.

## The Death of War

*A Vision of Arlington Cemetery*

On my gray grass hillside
Only rocks and flags will grow –
Lilacs, roses, cut and clinging,
Bow to sighs of wind and woe.

Lilies left to lace my walkways,
Violets, purpling twilight's glow –
All must wither as I watch them:
Only rocks and flags will grow.

## Epitaph on an Army of Amateurs

On sweating street and crippled swamp
        Brittle breaks the merry mist:
A ghost of soldiers groans for glee,
        Parade uncalled and lips unkissed.

Jungles creep their gauzy dream,
        Tendrils cling in green decay:
Lotus – orchid – *fleurs du mal*
        Enjoy the thought of judgment day.

Mounds abound and helmets bloom
        On stakes, with arms extended –
Asia oozes and contracts:
        Will, not war, is ended.

## An-drew Jackson: A Chant

I.

Andrew Jackson,
Hand-made hero,
Lion-maned, Samson-souled,
Out of a sun-spurned, rising West,
Out of the wild of man and god –
Dueller's coat with winding tails,
Aflap with black and a bullet's breath.

II.

Andrew Jackson,
Hand-made horror,
Corn-cribbed, hickory-hearted,
Honed and whetted to reap the wind!
Into the red-upholstered city,
Into the powdered, scented East –
Dueller's coat with whispering tails,
Aflap with the homespun smell of death.

III.

Andrew Jackson,
Hand-made, hallowed,
Boy-child graced with a soldier's scar,
Into the sabered slough of history,
Into the damasked seat of scorn –
Dueller's coat of many colors,
Aflap with fear and a nation's sigh.

IV.

Andrew Jackson,
Hand-made hero,
Rolled in battle blood, venom-varnished,
Late of the spoiling president's chair!
Odd the things your image graces:
Whiskey, statues, paper money –
Things as dead as the dueller's coat
And the tea-tipped tongues that stitched its lie.

## Gettysburg Field

Today I walked on Gettysburg Field –
Here the devil-dance locked its lovers,
Sainted Lee and forgotten Meade:
A nation bled itself to life
And kept this field to tell the tale.

Today I stalked the peach-sweet Orchard,
History-heavy, green with horror –
Cannon, crag, and wind-rocked wall –
Snake-rail fence, whose bayonet posts
Scratched at the sky and the South's gray cloud.

Today I stood where once Lee stood,
Who sent proud Pickett, the fair-haired South,
Who decked with young the smoke-stained altar:
Abraham yielding precious Isaac –
God's hand staying not the knife.

Today I moved where bronze-black faces
Still stare madness, ridge to ridge –
Red-tongued rifles rusting redder,
Monuments, mysteries, white with bloom,
As far Alleghenies run rich to the sun.

Today I dreamed in Gettysburg garden,
Grass as green as the youth that pressed it,
Flowers red as the blood that fell –
And I wondered then, could it really have happened,
Here in this field, this land, this world?

## Soonest Beauty: A Child's Funeral

I went to church to see my God,
A coffin on my knee;
The door stood wide, the lamp was lit,
But no God could I see.

God came to my house that same day –
To see me, I suppose.
I wasn't in; he didn't stay,
But left for me a rose:

A rose as red with sweet and thorn
As ever mortal saw.
Its bloom has passed – like God, like me –
Its bloom, its only flaw.

## Early and Late

Can my heart be broken, Father,
Ere I be a man?
Aye, in many pieces:
Mend it if you can.

But if I cannot, Father,
Then what shall I do?
Why, wait, my son; drink deep, and wait,
Till broken it is anew.

## The Race Half-Finished

Have you won then, all my heart?
Shall I see you win no more?
Atalanta's end of appling! –
Have you found the other door?

Leave me then, my loss of losses!
To the swift the unending race.
Time remains forever timeless:
Earth in instants knows its place.

## We Danced on Waves of Ocean

We danced on waves of ocean,
      Drew honey from the stars;
We drank the wine eternal
      That covers mortal scars –

With all my life I loved you,
      With hope of life to come –
Till whited ash of loving
      Left lips and body dumb.

Nor was my substance wasted,
      Nor were my tears too few –
But truth was more than telling,
      And you were true to you.

## Whither, Shame?

Whither, shame, amid so many causes?
How to live the penance of our day?
How to count, much less redeem, our losses?

Time-hardened heart, our shield of many bosses,
We turn against whatever saviours say. —
Whither, shame, amid so many causes?

On endless seas of care our vessel tosses —
What new excuse will keep the Christ at bay?
How to count, much less redeem, our losses?

Earth's mighty music moves: it knows no pauses —
Man alone mocks time with precious play.
Whither, shame, amid so many causes?

The righteous rest beneath their hallowed mosses;
Lost lambs, unseen, forever die astray.
How to count, much less redeem, our losses?

Numb, we thread God's wilderness of crosses,
Healed of that disease which made us pray —
Whither, shame, amid so many causes?
How to count, much less redeem, our losses?

## The Stone

The gray rock greens, as if it grew!
But wind and weathers all too few
Have stained its stretch of careless face:
It holds no brief — it makes no case.

The stone lies bare of all intent
But to remember her who went
Beneath, with naught but love of one
Who would in vain outdo the stone.

## The Ironmonger's Laurel

Iron-green enamel blossoms
Swing in stately mock
Above the sterile wall:
Can the metallist
Have raised a crop
Where even God despaired?
Not often, in a mind
Gone dead with seeding,
Nature climbs to artifice
Through pounding fire.
How many hammers
Did the anvil break
Before such petals
Pushed through adamant?
How many years were yesterday
Before this graven image
Rose to star an empty sky?

## The Child at the Washington Zoo

On the street where I live,
Life leaks like a sieve –
The police are too frightened to play.

On the street where I live,
All take and none give;
And it's always the devil to pay.

On the street where I live,
Not a gun, not a shiv
But will, like a dog, have its day.

On the street where I live –
God forbid! God forgive!
I'll be glad when they cart me away.

## A Peopled Garden

It overgrew while I was gone,
The stony patch I call my lawn;
And though I labored half the day,
I could but drive the weeds away.

They will return, I shall depart;
And yet I bear them in my heart,
For are they not dear enemies? —
Who score my back, who bruise my knees,

Who teach me, like a debt unpaid,
That enemies are ever made
By innocent neglect of care —
So vegetably sure, they scare!

## Departed Grace

She speaks no more; nor could I bear
Her words ineffable, so near
To tumbril tears of hopelessness;
For life or death, or something less,
Has dulled the bright of morning star –
Has left the world as deserts are,
With dearth and din and dust returning.

No, the sound of skies afire
Has shrunk to whisper from the pyre
That music died and art has flown,
And laughter burns beneath the bone
To solace who can laugh no more –
As waning oceans kiss the shore
With shift and drift and graceless yearning.

## Where More than Rivers Run

The sea comes in *comme ça, comme ça,*
And never knows its home;
It wanders wide of any mark
And sings to God alone.

Sure death to drink, but life to feel,
To beat with hand or blade,
To conquer with presuming keel,
To white its wine-dark shade!

We know it not, nor ever can;
It stiffens to our gaze:
It ghosts and goes *comme ci, comme ci* –
It beckons and betrays.

## Poetic Coming of Age

The chastened hand lies cold and dumb
    That once created half a world –
Before its richest dreams grew white,
    It knew to blush where gardens girled.

Once it wakened deeper longing,
    Once it knew a father's state –
Once it shadowed hills of heaven,
    Once it opened passion's gate.

Once it worshipped, once it whispered
    Words unheard and thoughts unfeared;
Once it spoke a lover's language,
    Till its ghost in flesh appeared.

Now to sterile pen accustomed,
    Once it wrought in mortal fire –
Damned to dumb perfection now,
    It knows no longer to aspire.

## On the Death of My Mother, After Long Illness

So sun is set with you,
And darkness come! –
Where find the light?
Where find what once was home?

So deftly fell the stroke –
No stroke to you,
Who wished relief,
Nor looked for vistas new –

Who sought the gray God's gift,
And heard anon
The dying fall
Of life's long clarion.

Your gentle love Christ welcome!
Nor hope be lost
Of His, or yours,
My own, my holy ghost.

Part II.

# Responses, Wry and Reverent

## After Reading Yeats's "Spinning Song"

*"There are seven that pull the thread..."*

Yeats would have it seven,
But nine are they that pull –
Yea, nine and more! But nine
I know, like stars that grind
The night to golden dust –
And with the gloried Greeks
I seek their dooming touch.
Let them flay me, living,
With their holy knife!
The fate of Marsyas
Would soothe and sate,
If they but let me sing
Before I die.

## The Abishag Rag: King David's Final Song

*Now King David was old and stricken in years; and they covered him with clothes, but he gat no heat.*

*Wherefore his servants said unto him, Let there be sought for my lord the king a young virgin: and let her stand before the king, and let her cherish him, and let her lie in thy bosom, that my lord the king may get heat.*

*So they sought for a fair damsel throughout all the coasts of Israel, and found Ăb´i-shăg a Shu´nammīte, and brought her to the king.*

*And the damsel was very fair, and cherished the king, and ministered to him: but the king knew her not.*

*– I Kings 1:1-4*

O Abishag, where *is* my harp?
Where the willow of infinite tear?
On me God frowns, and on my brow
Sit all the snows of yesteryear.

Who will lift the fallen taper?
Who will kindle kingly fire?
Who will make the monarch caper –
Make the calendar a liar?

Waxing old and waxing wicked,
Sins and yens yet incomplete –
Heat in bedclothes? Yea, unwed clothes:
Now that's all there is in heat.

Who will sigh and who will simper?
Who will teach the hours to dance?
Who will cherish, ere I perish,
What Bathsheba left to chance?

O comely maid, O coastal virgin,
Fire that turns to day the night!
Who could warm the dead to life
But Abishag the Shunamite?

Alas, O Abishag, I falter,
        Worse than dead — beyond your touch:
Vain each sacrificial vow —
        I loved not well, but overmuch.

Oft in battle, oft in council,
        Carried I the day —and year;
Now, though none but you oppose,
        My kingdom for a loyal spear!

Noah had at last his vineyard;
        Cain found home and hope in Nod!
*I* am left a withered proverb:
        Spared the child—ah, spoiled the rod!

O Abishag, I lived too soon,
        I sang my songs before my time:
To me remains Methus'lah's curse,
        To you a leprous, 'strep'rous rhyme!

## The Ship Burial of Scyld Scefing

*Þæt wæs gōd cyning!*

*Beowulf*, 11. 26-52

Then, at the fated time, went forth
The noble Scyld to God's great hall.
Friends – his faithful – honored there
The charge he gave them while he ruled.
To ocean's edge retainers bore him,
Prince of peoples, long their lord.
Hard at harbor chafed his ship,
Ring-stemmed prow ice-gray and eager!
There, in the ship's waist, laid they him,
Lord and giver great of rings,
Belovéd man in glory garbed:
Weighted, burdened bright with honor.
Far-borne treasures heaped they then
Upon him, glory-great as he lay.
Nor have I heard of a fairer vessel,
Filled with spears, with war-forged weapons,
Shirts of mail and gleaming swords.
Upon his breast lay gold and gems
To journey far in the flood's full force.
No less did they then furnish him
With arms and gold, their people's treasure,
Than had the ancient ones, unknown,
Who in the black beginning sent
Him forth alone, a sea-borne babe.
A standard all of gold they raised
At last above his hallowed head:
Then suffered they the salt sea wave
To bear him off – gave up their lord.
Sad the heart of them, mourning-mad
Their every spirit. None can say,
To tell the truth – the wisest ones
Who dwell in hall, heroes breasting
Gray-girt heaven – none can say
To whom that holy harvest came.

## The Coming of Octovyen

*I asked oon, ladde a lymere:*
*"Say felowe, who shal hunte here?"*
*Quod I, and he answered ageyn,*
*"Syr, th' emperour Octovyen,"*
*Quod he, "and ys here faste by."*
*"A Goddess half, in good tyme!" quod I,*
*"Go we faste!" and gan to ryde.*

– Chaucer's *Book of the Duchess*

Why should a brindled calf lie down
When summer sun makes meadows young,
When lark and larkspur color clods
And cowslips' silent bells are rung –

When all the world can laugh alive
And slaughter yet is years away,
When only signs of purple time
Are broken bread and break of day?

Why should all that's flaming stop
And stretch itself and chew before –
Before horns split the hearing ear
And open autumn's chilly store?

## Alysoun

*A rendition of the medieval English lyric, "Alysoun"*

When April treads the heel of March
And flowers spring to life,
When songbirds over treetops arch
To sing their loving strife,
My days with sorrow rife
I owe my wished-for wife:
She cuts me like a knife!
I love too deep, too soon —
A handsome lot, I know, is mine:
God made her face on me to shine,
And turned my love from all her kind
To light on Alysoun!

Her fairest hair is gold as chaff,
Her brows are brown, her eyes are black;
Her face is lovely as her laugh,
Her figure full can nothing lack.
My castle she may sack!
Ah, lift me from the rack —
Let love, or break my back,
And end my tortured tune!
A handsome lot, I know, is mine:
God made her face on me to shine
And turned my love from all her kind
To light on Alysoun!

At night I toss in bed awake;
My cheeks have grown so pale!
For you, my heart's redeeming ache,
Such longing makes me fail.
No man can tell the tale –
So fair a form, so frail:
Her love, my Holy Grail!
She turns my night to noon.
A handsome lot, I know, is mine:
God made her face on me to shine,
And turned my love from all her kind
To light on Alysoun!

For wooing I all sleepless lie
In tears enough to drown,
Lest any steal my earth, my sky,
My hope, my heaven's crown!
I cannot bear your frown:
I fall forever down!
O fairest under gown,
Harken to my rune.
A handsome lot, I know, is mine:
God made her face on me to shine,
And turned my love from all her kind
To light on Alysoun!

## On El Greco's Baptism of Christ

What came in scalloped shining from the hand
Of John? — What living fire uprose, or fell,
To scar the world? — Could he have known, who felt
The drops upon his brow, the drops that were
His own — the green Gethsemane of tears,
The raveled riches, the becoming pain,
The thrust of thorn, of never-ending spear?
Amid that gold of penitential sky,
Amid those serried spheres of angel-kind,
On silken breath of wingéd music falls
The Spirit, blind with ecstasy to heal
The severed centuries — to rest on him
Whose blood beats ever to propitiate
The Soul of All. — Transfixed, the Baptist waits,
As does the world — while he, whose naked limbs
Enfold his mystery, kneels mute to live
The destined touch in richest innocence
Of time, of place, of flesh — of all but love.

## The Burghers of Calais

*On Rodin's statue of the Burghers,*
*seen near closing time in the garden*
*of the Musèe Rodin in Paris, during*
*Christmas, 1956.*

Bronze-black Burghers, wind-worn, murmuring dark
Amid the Paris silence! — bare trees bend,
As angry evening snuffs the last long spark
Of whispered day — speak to a dreaming friend,
As statued twilight conjures dead Calais,
Ringed hard by bitter swords and queen-ruled king!
On hanging lips and arms vain questions play
Where one would reason to unreason bring;
Here shrugging silence pouts with mouth and hands
While there a hate-filled pride its moment lives;
But in that cirque of haltered hopes calm stands
A Christ, of deep-starved eyes, who yet forgives
And dreams, approaching death in quiet might,
Like a city, weary, welcoming the night.

NOTE. *According to Froissart's Chronicle, six citizens of Calais in 1347 volunteered to save their fellow townsmen from death at the hands of the then-besieging king of England, Edward III. The six citizens, or burghers, agreed to meet each of the English king's several demands. After presenting Edward with the keys to their city, they offered themselves up to his hangman, "stripped to their shirts with their hands and feet bare and a cord around their necks." Happily, the English queen interceded for them with her husband and caused them to be spared. As Froissart says, "She softened his heart, for she was pregnant."*

## On Jerome Bosch's Painting, "The Temptation of Saint Anthony"

By what dark right, O grimly wondering Saint,
Could human hands aspire to such a task,
To raise through mortal means an angel's plaint
And frame the question suns were born to ask?
Here horrors rush where living hope has fled,
And there in nightmare hues a chaos seethes
With awesome forms about your shrinking head:
An ever-tempting doubt its sickness breathes
That moves the earth in all of us to quake
And melts from Job to Judas souls most stout.
Unanswered questions, dwelt upon, must make
Of all God's art a wild, fantastic rout!
Then better far an ignorant bliss profess,
For still the righteous suffer righteousness.

## To Shelley

When clouds their watery whiteness change to black,
When moons and star-filled skies a yellow death
Have died, and west winds, tired, shall pant for breath
While waveless oceans slowly dry and crack –
When night no more heals wrong which day has done,
When blood-stained thorns of life no longer show
How redder yet the nearby rose must grow,
When nature's living Many must die One –
Then, Shelly, none shall scan your teeming verse,
Vast temple to all-seeing Plato raised.
And beauty then shall know the lonely curse
Of being undiluted though unpraised –
Like all the coins that cram philosophy's purse,
Unspent! – though moth and rust be sore amazed.

## On Thomas Hardy's "The Oxen"

On Christmas Eve, as night dies out
        And day by the clock begins to break,
Warm within and cold without,
        Hardy's Oxen stir and wake

To kneel again, as once they did,
        There, where the deed of God was done –
When all was clear and nothing hid,
        Gift and giver becoming one.

And something rises, like the tears
        That flow for reasons never known,
To blur the earth and all my years
        And make me see the manger throne.

Then sleep comes gentle, if at all,
        With what a mortal yet may feel! –
My pillow now the hallowed stall,
        And I arise but there to kneel.

## French Capital: The First Kiss of Love

If ever mere mortals were blessed from above,
The sexes made one without push, without shove:
The voice of the turtle, the din of the dove! –
  Lord Byron, you guessed it:
    The first kiss of love!

The moon was our minion, the sun dared not move:
All Paris was burning, our pleasures to prove –
Oh, mortise! - ah, tenon! - oh, tongue in its groove! –
  O Venus, you blessed it:
    We kissed in the Louvre!

By strand and by stream, through forest and grove,
Wherever, whenever two lovers might rove –
On stairway, in attic, like furnace, like stove,
  We tried to digest it,
    Our first kiss of love!

We did as we shouldn't; we mightily throve:
We made us an idol more monstrous than Jove!
We passioned, we fashioned a "flesh" treasure-trove:
  No pagan could best it,
    Our first kiss of love!

Yet a moment it lasted, that Tuesday so Shrove:
Grim Lent, with its fasting, too quickly uphove!
But as meat to the bone we heretically clove;
  We never confessed it,
    Our first kiss of love!

Though at last Time around us his tentacles wove,
As against his encroachments we valiantly strove –
Though the punishment fit us, as hand to the glove,
  I pray but God rest it,
    Our first kiss of love!

## On Robert Frost's "Provide, Provide"

The poet says, "Provide, provide!"
And so we hear on every side.
But what? How much? And is there time? –
Has trust in God become a crime?

Such worldly wit the Saviour loathed –
Bade none take thought how he'd be clothed,
Or how be fed, or paid, or treated,
Or, when at table, where be seated.

Must we "put money in our purse"
And live beneath Iago's curse?
Your "friendship bought"! The crowning straw
For camel's back already raw!

"Provision," if it blinds, cast out!
At least it's ours, the stroke, the gout,
The last long agony alone:
It's like the Saviour's – all our own.

Perdition take provision's pride:
Let live and let the grave provide!

## On Jenny as Bad Penny

*After reading Leigh Hunt's "Jenny Kissed Me"*

Jenny kissed you, say you so?
    Well, she's kissed a hundred others —
Would have kissed a hundred mo',
    If the wench had had her 'druthers.

Slander time and call him "thief"!
    Is shorter life a cause to mope?
'Tis weary — sad — and rarely brief:
    If time's a thief, then I'm the pope.

Jenny kissed you! "Cursed" is better:
    Deeds and dreams are not much like.
Sparks the steel when flint can whet her!
    Take your time — and take a hike.

## Reflections on the Book of Job

"The Bible hath no error" –
(Though Homer nods, like most) –
But *Job*'s as full of terror
As a tomb is full of ghost.

"Whence comest thou, Sir Devil?
Where hast thou been the while?"
"O'er all the earth I travel:
I stalk it, mile by mile."

"And hast thou yet considered
My perfect servant, Job? –
The worthiest of mortals
To wear an angel's robe!"

"Thy gloating is a caution!
Doth Job fear God for naught?
With home and flocks and fortune
Hast thou a servant bought."

"Believe it not, thou cynic!
Job loveth God for God –
And will, whatever cometh,
Good fortune or the rod."

"But touch him – take his treasure! –
Recall thy many gifts,
And Job will show 'his worship'
A plague of mortal shifts."

"Take thou and touch him – *thump* him! –
But spare his life, thou clod.
I keep my hand upon him,
And Job will keep to God."

"Agreed! Thou hast a wager!
'Twill quit us, thee and me:
From here to Ursa Major
God lieth! – all shall see!"

Well, Job went through the wringer,
And God went through the roof –
And what remains of Satan
Puts man to precious proof.

By all accounts, God whipped him –
But guess who kept the books:
When preachers plumb the porridge,
It's hell on heathen cooks.

"Whence comest thou, Sir Devil?"
As if He never knew!
God's best is seldom level,
And proofs are pesky few.

Who "carries" more than "cashes"
And trusts to love alone
Gets left among the ashes,
A thing of boils and bone.

To love God is to fear Him;
To leave Him is to die –
But try to get too near Him,
And you'll regret the try.

Be moderate in your virtue:
Play down the righteous rôle,
That Satan may not hurt you
Or God promote your soul.

Good works indeed hold promise
Of far more thick than thin,
But thank your lucky Thomas
That doubting is no sin.

And when some preacher offers
A "mansion" yet to bloom,
Be happy in your coffers –
A ghost that's full of tomb.

## 'Mid Evil Winters

*After reading Thomas Hardy's "Winter in Durnover Field"*

Bishop:
Across the board I find no rest,
As square askew the game goes on.

Peasant:
What *should* you find? Are you more blest
Than hobbled horse or pushing pawn?

Bishop:
Diagonally, I think, is best:
Direct is for the latter dawn ...

Castellan:
*Dieu vous regarde* with pox and pest!
To hear you talk –

Queen:
It makes me yawn.

Castellan:
There must be some more fruitful quest!

King:
That I could bid you all begone!–
But death is not for me to test.

Bishop:
As square askew the game goes on, ...

Castellan:
In rank or file or box, no rest! –

Queen:
Across the board we're put upon.

## His Coy Mistress to Him

*An answer to Andrew Marvell*

Had we but time enough and world
This boldness ('twould befit a churl)
Might do, indeed, for such as you –
Though such, thank God, are precious few.
Sit down and think which way to walk? –
As much a bore as try to talk!
The Ganges? Humber? Flood? The Jews?
Go try them on the tragic muse.
Your *vegetable* love? Good God!
'Twould rot the vine and salt the sod.
A hundred years to praise my eyes!
Why not begin about my thighs?
That's where you'd like to come to rest,
"Lip service" paid each budding breast.
To every part, you say, an age,
Then "put the parrot in his cage"?
Good sir, though such be my desert,
I'd rather sleep with snakes begirt.
 I wonder how you have the time
To hear a chariot or a chime
With all your fears of deserts vast,
Eternity, and ages past.
My beauty, ah, though never found
In marble vault or underground,
Will have to be its own reward
For me, for worms – may't please the Lord! –
So long as you, with all your crust,
Don't make it food for mortal lust.
The grave's a final, public place:
The *only* one where we'll embrace.
 Now therefore, while you're young and hot,
Go tell the world what I am not.
And while your itching flesh conspires
To make for maids their funeral pyres,
Go sport with trollops: croon and crow,
A coxcombed, barnyard gigolo.
Roll your strength like marijuana
In a smoke to make you fonder –
Tear your pleasures through the gates
Of idle girls with addled pates.
Thus, though I cannot make you run,
I'll sure as hell not bear your son.

## The Fiddler of Virginia

*Inspired by W.B. Yeats's "The Fiddler of Dooney"*

My brother's a surgeon in Richmond;
    My cousin, a broker of note;
I make my believe with a pencil –
    Regret not a line that I wrote.

My brother, my cousin, they passed me:
    They labored like saints of the kirk;
I dug and I delved like a sexton,
    But nobody thought it was work.

When the three of us come to a judgment
    And the Chap in the heavenly chair,
He will shake by the hand the two others –
    Me He will grab by the hair.

"Labor's the joy of my creatures!"
    He'll shout as he gives me a jerk:
"Ask of your brother and cousin –
    They bettered the world for their work!"

And the dreamer – the doubtingest Thomas –
    When he sees me slung to my nook,
Will sing out, "*Te deum laudamus*:
    If *he's* taken, God was sure took!"

But the best of a dream is believing:
    A poem can never be wrong.
The weavers of words are the mighty,
    And heaven is had for a song!

## From the Miller's Tale:
## Dame Aliso(u)n, "The Carpenteris Wyf"

*Chaucer,* The Canterbury Tales, *ll. 3221-3270*

This carpenter had newly wed a wife,
And her he seemed to love more than his life;
Eighteen she was, and for her tender age
Her husband kept her like a bird in cage.
So wild she was, he sighed (and sometimes chuckled),
"She'll play the devil making *me* a cuckold!"
He knew no Cato, or he read him wrong,
How evil wives to evil men belong,
And one should marry, if he does so late,
A wife too old to primp and agitate.
But since in his own trap he had been caught,
He must, like others, milk the cow he bought.
Fair was this young wife and altogether
Sleek as any weasel in the heather.
A sash with silken slashes wrapped her 'round
Above an apron, white as any found.
Thus warmed and covered were her lovely loins,
And on her smock there gleamed, like golden coins,
Embroidery before, behind, beneath;
Her silken collar, like a coal-black sheath,
Enclosed her supple neck and matched the shade
Of cap and ribbons which adorned her head.
She wore the cap with headband cocked awry, –
And bless us, but she had a lecherous eye!
Well-plucked and lined and black as hellish pitch,
Her arching brows might make the devil itch!
She was indeed a wondrous sight to see,
More round and red than apples on a tree.
And yet her skin was soft as virgin wool –
Good substance over husbands' eyes to pull.
Beside her hung a leather purse, with silk
And pearl adorned, as white as mother's milk.
No drunken dreamer on a garden bench
Could boast his fevered mind saw such a wench!
Her cheeks and coloring were ever sunny:
She glowed all over, bright as new-made money.

Her singing was as smooth as carded yarn,
And sweet as any swallow's in the barn.
And she knew how to skip and prance and bow
Like half a dozen calves behind a cow.
Her breath was sweet as mead or honeyed ale,
Or apples fast-fermenting in a pail.
Frisky was she as a new-born colt,
Or as a bird in spring about to molt.
Her brooch and blouse she never seemed to doff,
Though many would have helped her take them off.
Her shoes she liked to lace up to her thigh:
A primrose path for saint or sinner's eye!
She was a prize for any lord to lay,
Or for some strapping farmer's wedding day.

Part III.

# Greek and Roman Graces

## Socrates' Prayer

*Based on the conclusion*
*of Plato's* Phaedrus

Belovéd Pan, ye spirits all
Who haunt this sacred place –
Grant beauty in my soul to me
And, outwardly, the grace
To live at one with beauty, and with thee.

Teach me, who on thy mercies call,
That wise is rich, and fair:
Only so much of gold give me
As temperate men can bear –
And as can bear one temperate man to thee.

## Cato's Creed

*A blank-verse rendition of the lines from M.A. Lucanus' Latin Epic,* [The] Civil War, *which set forth the speech of Marcus Porcius Cato, "Cato the Younger," at the temple of Jupiter Ammon in North Africa, where Cato is urged by his general, Labienus, to enter the temple and consult its famous oracle.*

What, Labienus, would you have me ask?
Whether battle-death in freedom's cause
Is not far better than to live enslaved?
Or, can this life itself, if rightly lived,
Hold greater worth by being long or short?
Should he whose virtue shields him fear such pain
As fortune yet may wreak upon his flesh?
Or, whether righteous will is not supreme,
And due achievement of intended good
Adds naught to one's initial dedication?
These things I know; nor need I soothing word
From any gods but those to whom all men
Are bound – who utter forth our lives, though priest
And oracle be dumb – whose vision, voiceless,
Here seals our mortal deeds and days. To us
At birth the ancient author of the world
Laid open, once and ever, all we men
Shall know. Think you our god would deem these sands,
This desert waste where few can hear, a fit
Abode for him or his prophetic word?
What now – save all the elements: earth, air,
The sea, this fiery sky – what *can* our god
Inhabit? – *These* things still, and honest virtue,
In whomsoever found! Why seek we yet
The evidence of this, our deity?
He lives in all we see and do! I leave
Prediction to the doubters and the fearful.
No oracles for me! In death I find
My certainty – in death, the one thing sure
And common to us all. God's favored, god's
Despised – yea, hero, coward – all must die:
So Jupiter decrees. It is enough!

## On Translating Horace, Lord of Latin

Horace, how your work goes on!
We hacks and pedants sweat till dawn
To Anglify your silken meters:
You speak in pints; we gush in liters.
Daily, gaily you remind us
Latin *lives*! And you must find us,
In our labyrinthine tongue,
Striving, all, to keep you young –
To wear your spirit on our sleeve,
And make our heathen youth believe.
Come, teach us art's unending story:
Ours the labor, yours the glory!

## Invocation to Venus

*Horace, I Odes xxx*

O Venus, Queen of Cnidus and Paphos,
Leave your delightful Cyprian home:
Haste to the worthy shrine of Glycera –
        Her lavish incense calls.

With you, let come your zealous son,
The Graces, coolly dressed, and Nymphs,
Youth, Mercury – all little worth
        Without your loving self.

## Hymn to Diana and Apollo, Children of Jove and Leto (Latona)

*Horace, I Odes xxi*

O tender virgins, sing of Diana!
Youths, sing of unshorn Apollo,
        And Leto, deeply adored
                By Jove, most mighty of gods!

Praise her, lover of leaf-laden groves
And rivers, even on Algidus cold,
        In dark Erymanthine shade,
                On well-wooded Cragus the green.

Again, praise Tempe and Delos, isle
Of Apollo's birth, and praise the quiver,
        His sign, and his brother's gift,
                The lyre, blessing his shoulder.

Tear-stained war, vile famine and plague
Let him drive from Rome and Caesar, its lord,
        Away upon Persians and Britons –
                Moved by your praiseful prayer!

## O Fons Bandusiae

*Horace, III Odes xiii*

O spring of Bandusia, brighter than glass,
Sweet-wine worthy, not without flowers,
        Tomorrow yours shall be
                The kid, whose brow abloom

With horns foretells both love and war
In vain! – For he your icy streams
        Shall dye rich-red with blood,
                This child of the lusty flock.

Searing August cannot touch you:
Ever-cheering cool you give
        To oxen, plough-weary,
                And all the wandering herd.

Be now among the famous fountains,
While I sing of the ilex high
        Above those hollow rocks
                Your laughing waters bathe.

## Integer Vitae

*Horace, I Odes xxii*

Whole of life and free of wrong,
        One needs no Moorish spears,
Nor quiver, Fuscus, laden down
          With poisoned shafts,

If go he must through boiling Syrtes,
        Barren Caucasus,
Or through those lands the famed Hydaspes
          Lives to bathe.

For, as in Sabine wood I strayed
        Beyond my bounds, unarmed,
And sang of Lalagë, my own,
          A wolf fled me!

Apulia, with its soldier-oaks,
        Nurtures no such monster —
Dry Juba, nurse of lions, could
          Not breed his like.

Put me in deserts where no tree
        Feels any rising breeze,
Some end of earth beset by mists
          And blackest sky,

Or close beneath the sun in land
        Denied to human homes:
My love for Lalagë — sweet voice,
          Sweet laugh! — shall live.

## Augustus Caesar's Homecoming

*Horace, III Odes xiv*

Men, Herculean Caesar seeks
The gods of home! A deathless fame
At risk of death now won, he comes
        In victory from Spain!

Exulting in her peerless man,
Let her, his wife, do sacrifice
And join our noble leader's sister,
        Decked as suppliants.

O matrons and our children, saved,
And you young men and seemly maids,
Now thank just Gods, and speak no word
        Ill-omened or amiss.

For me, indeed, this festal day
Shall banish blackest care; while Caesar
Holds the earth, I fear not war –
        No, nor sudden death.

Go, fetch perfumes and flowers, boy,
And wine that saw the Marsian War –
If any jar by chance escaped
        Marauding Spartacus!

And bid sweet-voiced Neæra haste
To comb and bind her dark-brown hair!
Her hateful porter! – if he offers
        Hindrance, come away.

Graying hair makes mild the heart
Once all for fight and foolish quarrel –
In my hot youth, when Plancus ruled,
        Such slights I never bore.

## To Pyrrha

*Horace, I Odes v*

Amid so many a rose, what graceful youth,
Perfumed with fragrant oils, now woos you, Pyrrha,
In the grotto dear to you?
Your hair, so simply gold,

You bind for whom? How often will he mourn
Lost faith and fortune, and, unsolaced, stare
Upon his tranquil sea
Made black by bitter winds!

Who now enjoys and thinks you purest gold,
Who hopes to find you ever free and loving,
Knows not your treacherous storms!
O wretched all to whom,

Untried, you seem to glitter! Me the temple
Shows on sacred plaque, my wet clothes hung
As offerings to the lord
Most potent of the sea!

## Diffugere Nives

*Horace, IV Odes vii*

Now snows are fled and grasses green each field;
Bright leaves renew the trees;
All earth dons fresh attire, and rivers shrink
Within accustomed banks:
The graces, naked with their sister nymphs,
Lead out the dance of spring!
"Look not for life beyond the grave," say year
And hour, which steal the day.
Soft winds melt off the cold, and spring gives way
To summer, which must pass:
Rich autumn utters forth her fruit; then all
Feel winter's sterile cloud.
New moons make swift repair of heaven's ills,
Yet we mere mortals die:
For so did dutiful Aeneas, Tullus
The rich, and Ancus, famed.
We are but dust and shadow! Who knows? – will
Tomorrow grace today?
What now you grant your precious soul, Torquatus,
Alone escapes your heirs!
Once dead and Minos-judged, nor race nor right
Nor rhetoric will win
You life again: Diana cannot free
Hippolytus the pure,
Nor Theseus break the hellish chains that hold
His dear Perithoüs.

Part IV.

# Woolly Willy Speaks His Mind

## The Woolgatherer

You, with the eye of ocean gray,
With the look of age and the step of May,
With the stare and stoop and the bag so full,
Where do you gather your wishing wool?

"Why, here and there, and over beyond,
And off the edge of a moon-filled pond –
A-low where mole and spider school,
Aloft in heather, high and cool;
A briary birch oft gives its share:
Summer smiles it through the air! –
From fences free, from thrushes' nests –
Where caterpillars leave their vests,
Where a ghostly comet sheds its tail,
Where morning makes the star-mist pale –
Wherever I dream, wherever I am,
But never from a passing lamb!"

## Allah the Merciful

There's a lumbering line –
Some seventy years! –
Long as living, ugly as I,
Scrambling, scratching,
Humping, hatching –
Stretching far as the eye can see,
Back to the time when woe was me –
All of them waiting,
Mashing, mating,
Working their way,
Darkening day
And night
With their groans,
Picking their teeth
With each
Other's bones –
Pushing, pressing,
Never resting,
All of them crying,
All of them trying
To kiss my –
D'you think I'd let them?
Reader! Go
To the end of the line.

## Altared Sermon

Ol' Jake rasseled the angel there,
Under the ladder that come from heaven –
Held, and made the angel swear
Not seven, but seventy damned times seven ....

Ol' Jake rasseled and didn't know
The bargain he and his were makin' –
Slipped his skin and grinned his grow,
Got on with his commandment breakin'.

## Woolly Willy's Woman

Her moony face displays a wart;
    Her stature's squat, her temper tall –
But better 'tis to love a short
    Than never to have loved at all.

Her cooking hurts; her taste is vile;
    Her language withers uncut flowers;
Her nails repudiate the file;
    But what a harmony is ours!

She spits and spats; I let her rip;
    I drink when time and tide allow –
I'd like to put her on a ship
    And send her back to God somehow.

But well-a-day and heaven help! –
    And where to find the where-withal?
Far better love a lion's whelp
    Than never to have loved at all.

### To Name and Number the Twelve

The disciples are hard to decipher,
As into their numbers I delve:
At times they appear to be rifer
Than the usual deluge of twelve.
Old Peter the Rock: number one –
"Simon" before he was tapped –
Then Zebedee's Jamie and John,
Who were named for the thunder that clapped.
(Precursors of differing clergies,
They argued and fought all the day:
Thus known as the two "Boanérges,"
They made their mellifluous way.)
Now take a good breath and we'll start:
(To say them will make you feel stouter!) –
There's Andrew and Philip and Bart,
There's Matt and there's Tommy the Doubter;
(We've got only eight, but we're gainin'!) –
There's Jimmie (Old Alpheus' son),
There's Thad and there's Simon of Canaan,
And Judas, the terrible one.
That's twelve, and though rather too many,
They drummed up another ere long –
For Judas, the ever-bad penny,
Must needs be replaced for his wrong.
Matthias was chosen to do so:
As "apostle" he answered the call,

And labored like Robinson Crusoe
    To make a good "Friday" of all.
But "disciples" include not Matthias:
    The title belongs to the twelve;
And not an "apostle" is Judas –
    (He's one we would *all* like to shelve.)
And then there's the title of "saint":
    It's enough to make clergymen cuss,
For Aúgustine, under the paint,
    Is England's "apostle," Saint Gus.
And the Irish, of course, have their 'druthers:
    The "apostle" to them is Saint Pat,
While Barnie and Paul and some others
    Are "apostles" *and* "saints" for all that.
So I'm back, like an imp to his idol,
    With the twelve who were picked by the Lord:
They're the first and the most *bona fidal*,
    And they strike an umbilical chord.

## Almost Thanksgiving

When Eve and Adam danced the jig
Ere modesty was worth a fig,
        When fruit hung high,
        And you and I
Were future germs, or not so big –

When goodly beasts did fight and feed,
And bellies full made mock of greed,
        When all but wasted,
        Since untasted,
Knowledge flourished, safely treed –

Then was God a father true,
Whose blush was sun, whose tears were dew –
        Whose truth untold
        Made Satan bold
And all the world a groaning pew.

What little need of preachers then,
Of church, of brimstone – or of men!
        Had God forgot
        Instead of "wot,"
I might rejoice, a germ again.

## The Gray Moons of Morning

Mysterious His ways, I know;
He nods, and worlds incline –
He makes the monstrous lift its head,
The snake and gold to shine.

He makes the snow and night to fall,
He makes hot love grow cold;
He makes the ills of younger days
Seem sweet as we grow old.

He makes our sin original,
He makes His own obscure;
He tells the fish what word to pray
Before it takes the lure.

The many are the miserable:
So say the chosen few;
But wherein lies the happiness
The few would scare us to?

No beer, no skittle ever made
Can long appease the mind;
No good, or dreamed or realized,
Can satisfy mankind.

So live and love oblivion,
A bed at last secure –
Like guillotine and gallows,
Of every ill the cure.

And the red moon, the white moon,
The gibbous and the gray,
The mists of mighty morning
Will cheer us as we pray.

## Ambition

I long to live like ancient wine,
Maturing to the end —
Consumed when at my very prime,
Ere vinegar begin.

## On Getting Older

My sloth,
It grow'th.

## I Believe

Lonely, deserted, unwanted, forgotten,
We slither and slobber the by-ways of life —
Seeking the moon of the misbegotten,
Seeking the meaning of whore and wife,

Till the Almighty, the grace-giving father,
Master of moment, eternity, all —
Grinds to his bosom like prodigal egg shells
Meaning and moon and the things that crawl.

## Last Communion

Comfort cold as corpses' feet, that Christ
My wretched sins already bought with blood!
Why – if this bad bargain stands – make they
So hellish hard my everlasting exit?
And what unearthly good might *one* of mine –
If sins be thus divisible – do him?

## Comfort Ye

If eye offend you, pluck it out;
        If hand offend, why, cut it off:
Let never thought of imperfection
        Linger, lest it make you scoff.

Know that I created perfect;
        Know that all is good, and just –
Know that either love or hate
        Becomes as well primeval dust.

## Priorities Re-arranged

To love and leave is woman's game,
Said I, when Fortune frowned;
Faith and froth are all the same,
In woman's flesh fast-bound.

She gave my heart and hand a squeeze,
She kissed my stubborn brow –
Then left for silks and wine-lit seas,
As "custom doth allow."

I moped and swore, pronounced her whore,
And once the door was shut,
Got out my book and thumbed it o'er
To see who else was what.

But all I found were fickle folk
Who held me quite to blame –
Who bade me learn to take a joke
And play the "leaving game."

So now I'm old, a bachelor bold,
With never a wife to name;
And as my heart grows bitter cold,
I love the leaving game.

## Song of the Highly Placed Exec

*I like to reap where I've not sown,*
*To gather figs of thistles:*
*Else why should Christ to earth come down,*
*Or Paul compose epistles?*

I am Caesar *and* his penny,
(Earthy word for heavenly goal!) –
"Greatest good for greatest many,"
Yea, 'twas spoken of the soul.

I am Caesar *and* his penny,
Tribute paid and never paid –
Sacrifice is always nice,
On altar or on deathbed laid.

I, the Alpha and Omega,
Ask no pardon, count no cost,
Keep my books forever open –
Nothing ventured, nothing lost.

Dust thou art, but dost thou know it?
Hardly! I am not so hard:
Bliss at work is not to blister –
I would not the dumb retard.

Learn to work for what is given:
Strike nor boycott prospers here –
For good the crown is rest in death,
For sin the wage is living fear.

Eat and drink, but be not merry;
        Spend, be spent, and reproduce!
Tarry not to wonder why —
        No profit comes of things abstruse.

Naught but labor be your faith,
        Nor even darkly search the glass —
Do unto all as I do you,
        And know that even this shall pass.

*I like to reap where I've not sown,*
    *To gather figs of thistles:*
*Else why should Christ to earth come down,*
    *Or Paul compose epistles?*

## Cupid's Song

I come to turn your life to love,
To all its cheer and chances,
To its "below," not its "above":
To all its earthy fancies!

I ask no more than to be used
By king and priest and peasant –
To raise the dead and self-abused,
And make the worst seem pleasant.

I long to shake 'neath every sheet,
Chemise, culotte, serape –
A lover make of all I meet,
And make each lover happy!

## The Next-to-Last Ditch

Home is the seer of wonders,
Predator mind with its kill –
Home is the weary of travel,
Home is the heart never still.

Home is the dream and the dreamer,
Rites of passage behind –
Harlequin wrapped in forever,
Fit now for leading the blind.

## Wookles and Soolins

A wookle there was, both sober and true,
Who had him a soolin, as most wookles do;
And he said to his soolin one morning for pay,
"We can't go on living this fooliber way!

"We must off to the whistle of day in the wind,
Where night never dawns, and none ever sinned,
Where work is all done and the drinks are all mixed,
And naught comes a man and his craving betwixt –

"Where the hills are prodigious, and valleys between
Are monstrously deep and of billiard-cloth green,
Where the somber and solemn are banished forthwith,
And wry are the currents of moment and pith –

"Where the poor are all kings and the kings are divine –
There's nothing that's yours or that's theirs or that's mine –
Where thoughts are all golden and mothers are pearl,
Each wish is a horse, and each mule is a girl –

"Where spring is forever – eternity's now!
And none but an Indian dares to say 'How?'" –
Then the soolin looked glum, and "If all that is true,"
Said he, "what remains for a soolin to do?"

But the wookle, who valued his soolin most much,
Had surely not dreamed of a thing that was such!
For over the end of his wookly nose
There trickled a tear like dew on a rose,

And "*Well!*" he said: "Bless us! Why, what do you think!
Good heavens! I never –! Just fetch me a drink!"

## The Riddle

What is it, comes like Christmas,
And goes again like May,
And teaches in its passage
That two or more can play –

That brings a warmth to winter,
A tear to summer's eye –
That leads us not to tempting,
But heaven, if we try?

What is it, cool as morning,
That heats us like the noon,
And gives us solemn warning
That late is none too soon?

What is it, makes us merry,
And makes us sad besides –
That slows the Stygian ferry
And turns the head of tides? –

That fills the wise with wonder,
That blesses king and churl?
The world indeed should ponder:
I would not shame the world!

## Animal Spirits

Of animal spirits I'm fond:
May they people the Great Beyond!
    And if they do not,
    I'm back at a trot
To the slough of the Now and Despond.

If I catch me a roving rhinoceros,
I'll paint him all over with phosphorous
    And show him abroad
    As a horse dinosaur-ed,
Or a Byzantine pope from the Bosphorus.

Oh, the truth of an elephant's trunk
Is never a thing to debunk:
    He can hose with the best,
    He can nose with the rest,
And he's sober when most he has drunk.

Well, the leopard's a creature of parts –
He prances in fits and in starts;
    Wherever he found 'em,
    His spots (you can count 'em!)
Are cream of *couturier* arts.

Hippopotamos – riverine horse!
Without you, incredible loss:
    You remind us of ships
    And of women with hips
And Creators with humor, of course!

Was ever a wiggle so wary
As the neck of a spry dromedary?
	It gives you the quakes
	Like a bucket of snakes
And leaves you a bit *mal-de-mer-y.*

A humorless beast, the giraffe!
He runs like a crippled carafe;
	But he never gives wine,
	He can't even whine,
And no one has known him to laugh.

Now a Lab, though the dog with the most,
Has manners too muddy to boast:
	He'll lick you to death
	With a buzzardy breath,
But the coldest of hearts he will toast.

I never saw a unicorn,
	Nor do I hope to see one;
But sure as you and I are born,
	I'd rather be than see one.

Part V.

# Some Legends of Virginia

## Jack Jouett's Ride: An Episode of the Revolution

*Fateful June of 'eighty-one –*
*Tarleton hoped to have some fun:*
*Dragoons and British infantry,*
*Horsed and huffed with regal pride,*
*Struck for the heart of Piedmontry –*
*They reckoned not on Jouett's ride!*

Plume and mane flew up and down
As out they rode from Richmond Town –
Never a thought of Fortune's frown,
Or how one man could do them brown.

Out they rode with a fiery flare
On local horses stolen there:
Virginia's best, both colt and mare –
Thoroughbreds of more renown
Than those who sat them, I'll be bound!

*A hundred and eighty stout dragoons,*
*With many a mounted grenadier –*
*They marched to Hanoverian tunes*
*And the scheming dream of a British peer.*

Out rode Tarleton's little horde
Sent by England's learnéd Lord
Cornwallis – he of dubious fame
Who lived to lose the Yorktown game –
Out and off with never a fear:
The best King George could field that year,
Seasoned fat by British beer.

Out they rode on Charlottesville:
Virginia's great, for good or ill,
Had thither fled to fight on still
For home and hearth and freedom dear:
Some thought it would not last the year.
(The British thought it long had died –
They reckoned not on Jouett's ride!)

Smoke and smirk of 'eighty-one!
The seventy miles were well begun:
Evening came, that June the third,
And Tarleton rode with never a word
Of why or whither his horse he spurred.
Banastre Tarleton, Satan's kin,
Jounced along with a jingling din –

Never let on where he was bound,
North or south, or all around!
"Hunting Leopard" the British called
This raider-colonel, never appalled
At shot or shell that grazed his head:
No heart of his would e'er be bled
By war or woman — so he said;
No need had he of aught but force,
No wanton wit, no vain remorse.
Boots and pistols all a-shine,
He gazed with pride along his line
And dreamed of triumph soon to come,
Virginia's great beneath his thumb —
Thomas Nelson, Richard Lee,
Patrick Henry (they're but three!),
Jefferson, Walker, more besides:
The Legislature, the people's guides —
Statesmen all and heroes, too,
Men of old whose grit was true,
Who bore the Revolution's weight
And asked of God no finer fate.

The road ran out Louísa way;
Beside it Cuckoo Tavern lay,
And there, at almost ten of the clock,
Bar and bottle began to rock —
Shelf and table, cup and crock —
With the long-drawn thumping, rolling shock
Of heavy horse hooves pounding hard
The westward way none thought to guard.
Young Jack Jouett left his ale,
Eyed the column, head to tail,
Cursed and counted every gun —
His soldier-brother died by one! —
And what could *these* be set upon?
Bayonets, swords, and horses blowing:
Jouett guessed where they were going.
What but Jefferson's home lay west,
Forty miles from here at best? —
Governor, clerks, and all the rest
Who fled the east, when Richmond fell,
To make for Charlottesville pell mell!

Jouett, horseman, hunter too,
Asked of no one what to do –
Climbed his own great thoroughbred,
Whose mighty frame and thunderous tread
Made him lord of wood and heather:
Mouth of satin, lungs like leather,
Seventeen hands and a trifle more,
Bred to run, but he fairly tore!
Jouett and he made a handsome pair,
The horse dull black, the rider fair
With chest of oak and limbs like roots,
Six-feet-six in hunting boots;
Heavy but handy, strapping, sound,
He weighed two hundred, if a pound.
Tonight would see his hardest ride:
Coat and canteen cast aside,
And on his head the three-cocked hat
Whose feather flared like a flying bat!

The British held to the travelled road:
Moon at midnight clearly showed
Both bridge and ford and beaten way. –
Jouett rode through wheat and hay,
Through wood and gully where foxes play,
O'er hill and hummock never seen
Except by men in hunting green –
Meadows dark and ways uncouth
(All known to Jack since early youth) –
A shorter, harder road to ride,
But one that fed his native pride
As landmarks, loved, rose up and went,
And neither he nor his horse was spent!

Tarleton sauntered west at leisure,
Thought his jaunt the purest pleasure –
Gave his men one three-hours' "rest"
To do what Brits always did best:
A wagon-train they came across
(Bound for South Carolina's boss,
Nathanael Greene) they looted quite –
Bad, but it cost them half the night.
Then fired and feasted, on they went,
Clowns in need of a circus tent,
Blundering through that red-eyed dawn –
"On to Monticello! On!"

Jouett rode and stopped for naught:
God's gift, the little time *he* bought!
Through Louísa's muck and marsh,
The footing foul – the heat was harsh –
On he pushed his lathered horse:
Uncharted paths, but straight the course
As only a good Virginian knew –
The swift Rivanna, forded through
At Milton, there below the mount
Where lived the man some called "the Count
Of Albemarle and 'Monti-chell'"!
Was *he* to grace a prison cell?

Jouett, gasping, reached him there –
Muddied clothes and matted hair! –
Called him out and bade him flee.
The governor packed a shirt or three
And "westward, ho!" he hauled his bacon:
Home, but not the fight forsaken! –
None too soon, for the foe was there:
Clarion clatter cut the air
As just to the east, at "Castle Hill,"
Thomas Walker felt the chill
Of British brag and Tarleton's will:
A good long halt of half an hour!
Jefferson had high time to scour,
As Jouett drove *his* jaded steed
The last two miles through waste and weed
To warn the rest at Charlottesville —
Where Tarleton's ghost may seek them still!

The birds had flown, or so had most,
When Tarleton came with all his host.
The Legislature? They convened
Far west at Staunton, safely screened
By Blue Ridge Mountains, steep and high,
Which never a Brit would dare come nigh!

The war went on – and Tarleton's lot,
Late to grasp at what was not?
For him a fate far worse than death!
Virginia laughed, at every breath:
"Cavalry colonel gone to pot,
From greedy gallop to starvin' trot!
British bombast put to school
By young Jack Jouett, a ridin' fool!" –

For so the tale went 'round and 'round
From Charlottesville to Richmond Town
From Blue Ridge height to Piedmont plain,
Wherever wit had aught to gain.

*Fateful June of 'eighty-one –*
*Tarleton found a "fiddler's" fun:*
*Dragoons and British infantry,*
*Horsed and huffed with regal pride,*
*Gone from the heart of Piedmontry –*
*Beaten back by Jouett's ride!*

## Ballad of the Ghost's High Noon

Midnight spoke and the iron stroke
    Echoed long through street and lane;
A "madman" newly dead awoke
    To walk the village green again.

But what could a soul delivered want,
    As towered bells struck out their peal?
A maiden cold with ways to haunt
    There came to dance a merry reel!

Long years before, they danced as one –
    Until he fell beneath her heel:
Crushed and cursed in every bone
    With all she could not see or feel.

He went his way; she married much –
    Learned late that riches have their price.
He limped his life, nor craved a crutch,
    And died as the maiden turned to ice.

A madman, so the village thought –
    So strange and devil-dark his ways;
But all for her his lamp went out
    And on him dawned his dungeon days.

So now she comes, if night allow –
    Lest any see her bless his grave;
A warm wind wipes her stony brow:
    She knows it not her former slave!

And there, as forty years before,
    The two together, moveless, dance –
And she regrets amid her store
    That riches overruled romance.

Midnight spoke and the iron stroke
    Echoed loud for all to hear;
The maiden shook, drew in her cloak,
    And wept to learn what she must bear.

## In Memory of the Confederate Dead

The hills are green, the Valley fresh,
The fields of barley gleam with sun;
Corn and cattle fatten free,
As children play at war for fun –
Virginia lives! Virginia dies!
Her epitaph, her finest son:
The nation-state shall be no more –
It's all with Lee at Lexington.

The years have passed; the cup has not –
The bitter tale is never done;
The curse of many-venomed war,
The gall of grave and chain live on!
The silent pride, the Roman heart,
The dream of triumph all but won –
As heroes sleep and maidens weep,
It's all with Lee at Lexington.

## Revelation March

*The Good Old Rebel's Dream of Armageddon*

When the last Confederate soldier
Lies asleep in Southern soil,
When the last of Southern widows
Finds her rest from tear and toil,
When years that have forgotten us
Are dead as we once were,
When trumpets raise the fallen,
And ghosts of glory stir —
What's left of world and wisdom
Will be heir to such a sight
As would put the Yankee army
In a First-Manassas fright:
The devil, like a dragon,
Will arise to lead his own —
Earthquake, fire, and thunder
Will he hurl at heaven's throne!
And Michael, great Saint Michael,
Will be backed against the wall —
Till he calls up Southern soldiers
For his partners at the ball.
Then men in gray will rally
As we did in days gone by:
The hosts of hell and Satan
Will we once again defy!

We'll whip the devil's army
Till there's nothing of it left:
We'll smite the mighty dragon
Till it hollers "Uncle Jeff!"
Then butternut and barefoot
We will march to get our pay —
A ragamuffin army
With its song of "Look Away!"
We'll march to highest heaven,
And it won't seem far at all,
To a glory unimagined
Since the day of Adam's fall.
Our pay will be redemption,
As we prayed and hoped it would!
We'll be mentioned in dispatches
By the God of all that's good.
The stars and flights of angels
Will come crowding 'round to see
As we pass in grand review
Beneath the eye of Bobby Lee.
The universe will tremble
When we give the rebel yell:
They'll hear it from the heavens
To the depths of Yankee hell.
And the Lord will smile upon us;
He will say to us, "Well done!

You have fought and bled and suffered,
    But you made the devil run.
Lay down your arms forever
    And receive your just reward:
You're the finest fighting army
    That has ever served the Lord!"
So we'll stack our arms and enter
    Where the valiant are at rest:
Each last Confederate soldier
    Shall be numbered with the blest.
His widow will embrace him,
    And his children, at his knees:
It'll be like Christmas furlough
    'Neath the old magnolia trees!
The Lord Himself will lead us:
    The Stars and Bars will wave,
And we'll live the ancient adage
    That says, "Glory hath no grave."
The milk of paradise we'll drink,
    And dine on honey dew,
As the finest fighting army
    Great Jehovah ever knew!

## To a Great Beauty, Dying Imperfectly Mourned

If she hadn't been pretty
And purred like a kitty
And burned with the fires she fanned –
If she hadn't gone swimming
When juleps were brimming
And suits were in less than demand –
If she'd covered her bases
And straightened her laces
And learned to say "No!" or "Unhand!"
*Ah, well,*
*But she never said "No!" or "Unhand!"*

If she hadn't learned dancing
And eyebrow enhancing
And how to make fools of the best –
Had she learned how to pickle
Instead of to tickle
And raise all the hair on your chest –
Had she studied and tarried
And not gotten married
A time or three more than the rest –
*Ah, well,*
*But she marred and she married the best!*

Had the fiddlers of old
Whom liquor made bold
Not moved her to gallops galore –
Had she deigned to have children
Instead of bewilderin'
A half-dozen husbands or more –
Had she not thought of sinning
As just the beginning
Of womankind's ten and threescore –
*Ah, well,*
*Of a whopping-good ten and threescore!*

Had she kept all her lovers
Outside of the covers
And not put herself to the test –
Had she learned how to care
Instead of to swear
Like a drill sergeant out of *Beau Geste* –
Had she prayed to the Lord
And never adored
That bulbulous creature, Mae West –
*Ah, well,*
*That fabulous figure, Mae West!*

Had she gathered around her
Three saints to the bounder
And learned to tell kings from the kinks –
Had she let herself blossom
And never played possum
Among all the wolves and the minks –
Had she ever learned golf
And been able to scoff
At all else that occurred on the links –
*Ah, well,*
*Whatever occurred on the links!*

Yet her beauty! – it shone
Like a cut to the bone:
She sparked, as she sparkled, all day –
And she never was "bad,"
Though she gave all she had,
For she took only love as her pay.
And the truth of it was
That she hated applause,
Though she let it not stand in her way!
*Ah, well,*
*But she let nothing stand in her way!*

Well, the church was nigh-empty,
The preacher, unkempty –
(She hadn't a cent to her name!)
And the matrons that were
Wouldn't let the men stir –
(For she *did* have a scent of ill fame!)
So the service looked lonely,
None mourned as her "only,"
And few, the broad-minded that came.
*Ah, well,*
*Too few, the broad-minded that came!*

But the creatures of cant
With their scurrilous rant
Should have paused, in their primping, to pray:
Their thoughts would have risen
Like flags at the mizzen
With God, not the devil, to pay –
And her men without fear
Should have knelt at her bier
To give thanks that she happened this way –
*Ah,* yes!
*To thank heaven she happened this way!*

## The Bishop's Drinking Song

*Almost to the tune of "Blow the Man Down"*

*As persons in all walks of life have drinking songs, why not bishops as well? I remember hearing some of these verses while I was growing up in Richmond, or trying to. Goodwin, Johns, Kinsolving, Meade, Peterkin, Randolph, Tucker, Whittle – all, I believe, are names of former Virginia bishops. (The families of Goodwin, Tucker, and Kinsolving number among them clerics, if not bishops, more than one.) On the evening here celebrated, most of the other worthies named were probably just visiting. Bishop Meade (in an obvious pun on the site of the Magna Carta signing) was called "Runny," I suppose, because of his tendency to "run on." Bishop Johns had to be called "Johnny"; and Bishop Billings (perhaps a Montanan; certainly not a Virginian) must have been a teetotaler. The rest, no doubt, appear for reasons of euphony, poetic license, or equality before the bar. (A "sidecar," incidentally – which seems to have been Bishop Carmichael's favorite – is a concoction of brandy, orange liqueur, and lemon juice.) Though little there is to be said for a sacerdotal binge, as Chaucer puts it at the end of* The Miller's Tale, *"god save al the rout."*

We Bishops went drinking,
And few were a-shrinking –
CHORUS: As Bishoprics come and Bishoprics go!
So here's how we boasted
And tippled and toasted:
CHORUS: Yo ho, and we'll stick to the devil we know!

"Well, here's to the party!"
Said Bishop McCartey –
CHORUS: As Bishoprics come and Bishoprics go!
"To the wedding at Cana!"
Said stout Bishop Dana –
CHORUS: Yo, ho, and we'll stick to the devil we know!

"'Twill get us to supper,"
Said lean Bishop Tupper –
CHORUS: As Bishoprics come and Bishoprics go!
" ... And keep us from slumming!"
Said good Bishop Cumming –
CHORUS: Yo ho, and we'll stick to the devil we know!

"With spirits be lavish!"
Said Bishop McTavish –
CHORUS: As Bishoprics come and Bishoprics go!
"It beats Sunday gruel,"
Said wry Bishop Spruill –
CHORUS: Yo ho, and we'll stick to the devil we know!

"It's good for the bustle!"
Said fat Bishop Russell –
CHORUS: As Bishoprics come and Bishoprics go!
"I'll surely not stand off,"
Said gruff Bishop Randolph –
CHORUS: Yo ho, and we'll stick to the devil we know!

"Don't water my whiskey!"
Said Bishop Zabriskie –
CHORUS: As Bishoprics come and Bishoprics go!
"A must for my middle!"
Said round Bishop Riddle –
CHORUS: Yo ho, and we'll stick to the devil we know!

"May Satan's mouth pucker!"
Said wise Bishop Tucker –
CHORUS: As Bishoprics come and Bishoprics go!
"To gin and my 'druthers!"
Said Bishop Carothers –
CHORUS: Yo ho, and we'll stick to the devil we know!

"Like hogs to the swillings!"
Said blue Bishop Billings –
CHORUS: As Bishoprics come and Bishoprics go!
"Don't give me too little!"
Said stern Bishop Whittle –
CHORUS: Yo ho, and we'll stick to the devil we know!

"My head is revolving!"
Said Bishop Kinsolving –
CHORUS: As Bishoprics come and Bishoprics go!
"It won't make us paler!"
Said red Bishop Taylor –
CHORUS: Yo ho, and we'll stick to the devil we know!

"Well, down with all liquors!"
Said old Bishop Vickers –
CHORUS: As Bishoprics come and Bishoprics go!
"To the gospel and Godspeed!"
Said quaint Bishop "Runny" Meade –
CHORUS: Yo ho, and we'll stick to the devil we know!

"It feeds a man's fire!"
Said Bishop McGuire –
CHORUS: As Bishoprics come and Bishoprics go!
"Well, back to the bar again!"
Said hot Bishop Corrigan –
CHORUS: Yo ho, and we'll stick to the devil we know!

"To singing like Lily Pons!"
Said young Bishop "Johnnie" Johns –
CHORUS: As Bishoprics come and Bishoprics go!
"I hear harps and woodwinds!"
Said both Bishop Goodwins –
CHORUS: Yo ho, and we'll stick to the devil we know!

"To a 'Sidecar' and cycle!"
Said Bishop Carmichael –
CHORUS: As Bishoprics come and Bishoprics go!
"Till the bells are rung backward!"
Said loud Bishop Blackford –
CHORUS: Yo ho, and we'll stick to the devil we know!

"Get on with your sinnin'!"
Said grim Bishop Grinnan –
CHORUS: As Bishoprics come and Bishoprics go!
"We'll drink till we totter!"
Said gray Bishop Potter –
CHORUS: Yo ho, and we'll stick to the devil we know!

"It mellows me brogue!"
Said Bishop MacHoag –
CHORUS: As Bishoprics come and Bishoprics go!
"Can't drink like I use' to!"
Said poor Bishop Brewster –
CHORUS: Yo ho, and we'll stick to the devil we know!

"Just double my shot,"
Said wild Bishop Scott –
CHORUS: As Bishoprics come and Bishoprics go!
"Then *I'll* take a triple!"
Said cute Bishop Whipple —
CHORUS: Yo ho, and we'll stick to the devil we know!

"I've drunk my last penny!"
Said sad Bishop Denny –
CHORUS: As Bishoprics come and Bishoprics go!
"Have a highball on me-o!"
Said easy Pope Leo –
CHORUS: Yo ho, and we'll stick to the devil we know!

"Let nothing seduce us!"
Said cautious Confucius –
CHORUS: As Bishoprics come and Bishoprics go!
"No liquor gets by us!"
Said laughing Pope Pius –
CHORUS: Yo ho, and we'll stick to the devil we know!

"Here's blood in your eye!"
Said Bishop MacTigh –
CHORUS: As Bishoprics come and Bishoprics go!
"Well, suck up, then, dammit!"
Said wily Mohammet –
CHORUS: Yo ho, and we'll stick to the devil we know!

"Get ready my rammer!"
Said Archbishop Cranmer –
CHORUS: As Bishoprics come and Bishoprics go!
"Then, here's till we meet again!"
Said sweet Bishop Peterkin –
CHORUS: Yo ho, and we'll stick to the devil we know!

FULL CHORUS: So fill up your glasses,
And don't mention masses!
Yo ho, yo ho, and a beer for the band!
Now none could do better
Than wish us the wetter!
Yo ho, yo ho, and the lifeboats are manned!
Then, whiskey *below*,
Where the bad bishops go!
Yo ho, yo ho, and the devil be damned!
And thus we all sang
Until matin bells rang –
Yo ho, gut and gullet be wonderf'lly crammed!
Our song it is done,
Like the Heidelberg tun!
Yo ho, and we've emptied each bottle to hand!
We've drunk with the best
And to hell with the rest!
We're 'Piscopal, whiskopal Lords of the land!

WE'RE 'PISCOPAL, WHISKOPAL LORDS OF THE LAND!

## Clinton Campaign Song, 1992: The Bonnie Blue Flake

*To the tune of the "Bonnie Blue Flag"*

1

We are a band of robbers:
We'll steal you blind as bats!
We're known throughout the Commonwealth
As "Clinton Democrats."
We've bought the blacks in Washington –
They'll help us thieve and prate:
And what was once a nation's pride
Shall be the darky state!
CHORUS: Hoo-rah! Hoo-rah!
Slick Willy beats 'em all!
The Jews and Japs and Chinamen
Will love his Southern drawl!

2

He likes to go a-travellin'
Wherever there's a scam –
(He travelled far from Arkansas
To side-step Viet Nam!) –
And now he tours the country
With his carpet bag of tricks,
A-bussin' Gore to glory
And himself back to the Styx.
CHORUS.

3

Al Gore, he loves the lawyers,
Their warts and torts and all:
He'd let their verdicts rise to God,
Their souls to Satan fall!
And Hilary and Gennifer?
Slick Willy's up to both:
His girls will hold the Bible
As he takes his latest oath.
CHORUS.

4

He says he's for the wilderness
        And full employment, too.
And what he takes will never break
        The backs of me and you!
He'll tax the rich and famous,
        He'll seize and squeeze 'em dry,
And make each starving Democrat
        A Caesar by and by!
CHORUS.

5

He did a job in Littlerock
        That left his state behind;
He'll do one on the country
        That'll blow the public mind:
He's all for debts and deficits
        And Deals forever New;
He'll make you pay like LBJ
        And skin your children, too!
CHORUS : Hoo-rah! Hoo-rah!
            Slick Willy beats 'em all!
        The Jews and Japs and Chinamen
            Will love his Southern drawl!

So comes THE END:
Let none pretend
To please the muse forever.
My thanks to you,
Who've seen it through,
This woolly, wild endeavor!